Nita Mehta's

Mother & Child
Cookbook

– Pregnancy and Childcare –

Nita Mehta's
Mother & Child
Cookbook
– Pregnancy and Childcare –

Nita Mehta

B.Sc. (Home Science), M.Sc. (Food and Nutrition), Gold Medalist

SNAB
Excellence in Books

Nita Mehta's
Mother & Child
Cookbook
– Pregnancy and Childcare –

First Hardbound Edition 2009

ISBN 978-81-7869-211-1

Food Styling & Photography: **SNAB** Excellence in Books

Layout and Laser Typesetting:

 N.I.T.A. ☎ 23252948

National Information Technology Academy 3A/3, Asaf Ali Road New Delhi-110 002

Published by:

SNAB Excellence in Books Publishers Pvt. Ltd. 3A/3 Asaf Ali Road, New Delhi - 110002 Tel: 23252948, 23250091 Telefax:91-11-23250091

Editorial and Marketing office:
E-159, Greater Kailash-II, N.Delhi-48
Fax: 91-11-29225218, 29229558
Tel: 91-11-29214011, 29218574
E-Mail: nitamehta@email.com
nitamehta@nitamehta.com
Website: http://www.nitamehta.com
Website: http://www.snabindia.com

Printed at:
MANIPAL PRESS LTD

Distributed by:
THE VARIETY BOOK DEPOT
A.V.G. Bhavan, M 3 Con Circus
New Delhi - 110 001
Tel: 23417175, 23412567; Fax: 23415335
E-mail: varietybookdepot@rediffmail.com

Contributing Writers :
Anurag Mehta
Tanya Mehta

Editorial & Proofreading :
Rakesh
Ramesh

Price: Rs.

Introduction

*M*otherhood is the most wonderful gift nature has bestowed on women. The birth of your little one makes you enter a new phase of life; one that is both rewarding as well as challenging.

This book is divided into three broad sections: Pre Natal (Pregnancy) Recipes, Post Natal (after Child Birth) Recipes and Food for Your Baby.

The first section of the book guides you through your pregnancy, with recipes for a healthy pregnancy and child birth. The second section has recipes which would help you to replenish nutrient stores in your body and also give you the energy to recover from the stress of pregnancy and child birth. The third section is for your baby. It has recipes for a 4 month old to a 3 year old child, which help in healthy growth.

All the recipes have been created with utmost care to help you and your child have a nutritionally sound diet. The recipes given in the book can be enjoyed by the whole family as they are really delicious besides being very healthy. Hence, we decided to have the recipes serve more than one. Besides recipes, the book also has a lot of useful information which helps to clear the doubts of new mothers.

Nita Mehta

ABOUT THE RECIPES

WHAT'S IN A CUP?

INDIAN CUP
1 teacup = 200 ml liquid
AMERICAN CUP
1 cup = 240 ml liquid (8 oz)
The recipes in this book were tested with the Indian teacup which holds 200 ml liquid.

CONTENTS

Introduction   5

Eating for a healthy baby   8

Commonly asked questions...   10

Foods to include in your diet during pregnancy 12

Pre Natal Recipes   13

Red Bean & Chickpea Salad   14

Low Cal Choker Tikki   16

Oat-Moong Toast   18

Walnut & Broccoli Soup   20

Spinach Orange Salad   21

Subz Paneer Jalfrezi   22

Tomato-Kaju Idli   24

Saag Murg   26

Breakfast Platter   28

Achaari Broccoli & Kaddu   30

Spiced Paalak Roti   31

Wheat Bran-Soya Roti   31

Vegetable Chaat Nuggets   32

Post Natal Recipes   34

Healthy Measures After Child Birth   35

Commonly Asked Questions...   36

Porridge with Dates & Bananas   37

Nutty Banana Smoothie   37

Spicy Vegetable Dalia   38

Broccoli Mayo Wraps   40

Tomato Fish   42

Banana Berry Shake   43

Egg Cups with Broccoli   44

Panjiri   46

Food For Your Baby   77

Food for the Baby as per Age   48
More About Children's Food   49

Recipes
4 Months - 1 Year   50

Mashed Apple   51
Banana Pudding   52
Homemade Rice Cereal   53
Sooji Upma   54
Papaya Puree   55
Clear Moong Dal   56

Sweet Potatoes with Yogurt   57
Mango Masti   58
Semolina & Carrot Porridge   59
Lentil Khichri   60
Rice Phirni   61
Oatmeal and Bananas   62

Recipes
1 Year - 2 Years   63

Sprouty Peanut Tomato Rice   64
Corn Khichri   66
Banana French Toast   67
Soya~Lauki Puri   68
Spinach/Beetroot Cookies   69

Savoury Vegetable Dalia   70
Paper Thin Veggie Chips   71
Fresh Chikoo Icecream   72
Potato and Pea Curry   73
Cucumber Melts   74

Recipes
2 Years - 3 Years   75

Baked Chick Pea Rounds   76
Oat Fudge Fingers   78
Vegetable Tomato Pasta   80
Egg Rolls   81
Carrot Parantha   82
Spaghetti with Chicken   83
Besani Bites   84
Hero Hot Dogs   85

Savoury Potatoes   86
Besan Ki Burfi   87
Atta Besan Laddu   88
Pista Sandesh   88
Oat Ka Halwa   90
Nariyal Ki Burfi   92
Gajar Ka Halwa   93

Glossary Indian Names/Terms   94
International Conversion Guide   95

Eating for a Healthy Baby

During pregnancy, more than ever, it is essential that you have as varied and balanced a diet as possible. You do not need to plan this specially, nor do you have to eat for two. All you have to do is eat a variety of fresh, unprocessed foods, to ensure that you and your baby get all the nutrients you need.

IRON

Iron is absorbed more easily in presence of vitamin C, contrary to the tannin and caffiene present in tea and coffee which lower iron absorption. Avoid drinking tea or coffee immediately after meals, especially if you are a vegetarian since you cannot eat the most easily absorbed sources of iron.

Foods high in iron : red meats, oily fish such as sardines, poultry, eggs, spinach, cereals, pulses and legumes, dried fruits, olives, beans, whole meal bread.

PROTEIN

Protein helps to build, repair and replace the tissue, fights infection and helps in blood clotting. Animal sources are rich in protein, but are also high in fat, so limit your intake of these, and choose lean cuts of meat whenever possible. Avoid half/semi cooked or raw eggs and make sure all eggs you buy are fresh.

Foods high in protein : fish, meat, nuts, pulses and dairy foods.

FIBRE

Foods rich in fibre should form a large part of your daily diet since constipation is common in pregnancy and fibre will help prevent this.

Fruits and vegetables are important sources of fibre as you can eat a lot of them everyday.

VITAMIN C

It helps in building a strong placenta and fights infection, and also helps in the absorption of iron. It is found in fresh fruits and vegetables. Supplies of vitamin C are needed daily, as it cannot be stored in the body. A lot of vitamin C is lost by prolonged storage and cooking, so avoid prolonged storage & eat vegetables raw in the form of salads.

Foods high in vitamin C : broccoli, guava, green chillies, lemon & lime, orange, grapefruit, strawberries, capsicum, asparagus & tomato juice.

CALCIUM

This is important to ensure a healthy development of your baby's bones & teeth, which start forming around the eightth week. You will need about twice as much calcium as normal.

Foods high in calcium : cheese, skimmed milk, yogurt, leafy green vegetables, canned salmon, tofu, broccoli and legumes.

FOLIC ACID

Folic acid is a B vitamin that is needed for the development of the baby's central nervous system, especially in the first few weeks. Try to eat vegetables lightly steamed or raw.

Foods high in folic acid : spinach, broccoli, brussels sprouts, green beans, cooked kidney beans, chick peas, black beans, split peas, whole meal bread, breakfast cereals, hazelnuts.

ESSENTIAL FATTY ACIDS

These are vital for the development of your baby's brain, nervous system and retina.

Food high in fatty acids :Oily fish such as salmon and mackerel are the richest source. Nuts, seeds, whole grain cereals, and dark green leafy vegetables are other sources. Oils such as olive oil are rich in omega 3 fatty acids.

AVOID

SUGAR

Sugary foods, such as cakes, biscuits, jam, and fizzy drinks, are low in essential nutrients, & can make you put on excess weight during pregnancy. Try to get your energy from starchy carbohydrates, such as whole meal bread and pasta, and cut down on sweet things.

ALCOHOL

Avoid alcohol as it slows the absorption of folic acid which is a must nutrient for the baby. Alcohol has no nutrition and unneccessarily adds up empty calories.

Commonly Asked Questions...

Q. I am a vegetarian, how can I balance the nutrition content in my diet?

Ans. If you eat protein-rich foods like pulses, legumes and dairy products, you will provide the baby with all that it needs. The only nutrient you may lack is iron; the body has great difficulty absorbing iron that comes from plant sources, so you may be given supplements of the mineral to compensate. If you are a vegetarian and don't eat dairy products, you may also be prescribed calcium, and vitamins D and B12. Eat a lot of fruits and vegetables.

Q. Why should I restrict salt in my diet?

Ans. Excess salt is believed to be one of the causes related to problems such as swelling around the ankles and high blood pressure.

Q. Why do I get a heartburn after eating?

Ans. Fried foods, high-fat foods, refined sugar, chocolate, peppermint, spicy foods, citrus and caffeinated drinks cause heartburn, so avoid them. Instead of eating large meals three times a day, eat smaller meals more often if you suffer from heartburn.

Q. I love to snack in between meals. Should I?

Ans. There is nothing wrong with snacking during the day provided it is healthy. Healthy snacks will help you decrease morning sickness, give you energy and help provide that extra 300 calories a day required during pregnancy. Healthy snacks options: digestive biscuits or graham crackers, popcorn, pretzels, fruit, fortified cereal, raw vegetables and fruit smoothies.

Q. How to avoid morning sickness?

Ans. Snacking frequently and having lot of water help control morning sickness.

Q. **How to avoid constipation?**

Ans. Drink a lot of fluids and include foods high in fibre in your diet, such as whole-grain breads, beans, cereals and vegetables.

Q. **Do I need to avoid some types of cheese?**

Ans. Pregnant women should avoid soft cheese like Camembert, brie, blue cheese, feta and soft Mexican cheese like queso fresco and queso blanco. Cream cheese, however, is not considered to be a harmful for pregnant women.

Q. **What not to eat raw?**

Ans. Raw meat, poultry and seafood can put you at risk. Avoid mayonnaise, because it is prepared from raw eggs. Cook non-veg properly.

Q. **Why avoid processed foods?**

Ans. Avoid processed convenience food, such as canned foods and packet mixes. Processed foods often have sugar and salt added, and may contain a lot of fat as well as preservatives, flavourings, and colourings. Read the labels carefully and choose additive-free products.

Q. **Should coffee and tea be avoided? Any substitute for tea?**

Ans. Caffeine, a substance that is found in these drinks, has a harmful effect on the digestive system. Reduce your intake to no more than two cups of caffeine-containing drinks a day and if possible give them up altogether. Drink plenty of water instead. Herbal tea can be substituted for tea.

Foods to include in your diet during pregnancy

Following foods are excellent sources of at least one nutrient.

- Cheese, milk, yogurt — protein, calcium
- Dark green, leafy vegetables — vitamin C, fibre, folic acid
- Lean red meat — protein, iron
- Oranges — vitamin C, fibre
- Poultry — protein, iron
- Raisins and prunes — iron
- Sardines — protein, calcium, iron.
- White fish — protein
- Wheat bread — protein, fibre, folic acid
- Whole wheat pasta and brown rice — fibre

Fat taken moderately, is an important part of your diet.

JUST A POINT
Kick high fat and sugary snacks out of your diet—or at least limit them. Yellow fruits and vegetables are great sources of vitamin A in the body. Vitamin A helps maintain healthy skin, eyesight, bone growth and tooth development; enhances the immune system to help fight infection; and can reduce the risk of diseases.

PRE NATAL RECIPES

The recipes given in the book can be enjoyed by the whole family as they are delicious besides being very healthy. Hence, we decided to have the recipes serve more than one. During pregnancy, one feels hungry in-between meals. These snacks will take care of the hunger pangs and also make a healthy breakfast, which is the most important meal of the day.

Red Bean & Chickpea Salad

When you feel nauseated, this tangy mango chutney salad will change your mood.

Serves 4

½ cup red kidney beans (*rajma*)
½ cup chickpeas (*safeed/kabuli channa*)
1 cup grapes (black or green) or 1 cup peeled pieces of orange
1 small capsicum - thinly sliced
1 onion - thinly sliced
2 tomatoes - deseeded and thinly sliced

DRESSING
4 tbsp mango chutney (use ready-made or home made)
4 tbsp olive oil
1 tbsp honey
¼ cup chopped coriander leaves
1 tbsp crushed garlic
2 green chillies - chopped

1. Soak rajma and channa for 2 hours in hot water.
2. Put rajma, channa, 1 cup water and ½ tsp salt in a pressure cooker. Pressure cook to give 1 whistle. Reduce heat and cook for 4-5 minutes. Do not cook longer. Remove from fire. Let the pressure drop by itself. Drain.
3. Place boiled rajma, channa, grapes or orange, capsicum, onion and tomatoes in a bowl. Mix well.
4. Place all the ingredients of the dressing in a mixer and blend to a smooth puree.
5. Pour the dressing over the salad and mix well. Chill for 1 hour and serve.

Low Cal Choker Tikki

A good way of having wheat bran, which is the fibrous portion of wheat. Takes care of the constipation problem during pregnancy.

Makes 10

1 cup (40 gm) wheat bran (*choker*)
½ cup grated cauliflower
½ cup finely chopped spinach (*palak*)
1 carrot - grated
1 potato - boiled, peeled & grated (¾ cups)
1 green chilli - chopped
2 tbsp green coriander - chopped
¾ tsp salt, ½ tsp black pepper powder
½ tsp chaat masala
1 tsp lemon juice
seeds of 2 green cardamom (*chhoti elaichi*) - crushed
½ tsp honey
1-2 tbsp curd, approx.
1 tsp oil to brush the pan

YOGURT MUSTARD DIP (MIX TOGETHER)
½ cup yogurt - hang in a thin muslin cloth for 15 minutes
2-3 tsp mustard, according to your taste
¼ tsp each of salt, sugar and pepper

1. Mix together *choker* with all ingredients except oil and curd.
2. Add enough curd to *choker* mixture, to bind the mixture into balls.
3. Make balls. Flatten to form tikkis. Heat a non-stick frying pan, brush with a little oil and brown the tikkis on both sides on medium heat. Serve hot with mustard dip or hari chutney.

Oat-Moong Toast

*Pulse and oat batter - a very healthy combination, coated on bread and pan fried.
Serve it accompanied by hari chutney.*

Serves 2

½ cup oats - roasted for 2 minutes in a *kadhai*
¼ cup *dhuli moong dal* - soaked for 1-2 hours & ground to a paste
½ cup coriander leaves - chopped finely
½ tsp baking powder
1½ tsp lemon juice
1¼ tsp salt or to taste
a pinch of red chilli powder
4-5 tbsp oil
4 slices of brown bread

1. Drain and grind dal to a fine paste.
2. Mix moong dal paste, oats, coriander leaves, baking powder, lemon juice, salt and red chilli powder. Add water to make a thick paste of coating consistency.
3. Heat 4-5 tbsp oil in a non-stick pan.
4. Spread the oat mixture on one side of the bread slice with a spoon.
5. Invert the slice with the oat paste down in the hot oil.
6. Spread some oat paste on the upper side of the slice too, with a spoon. Turn. Shallow fry on both sides until light brown.
7. Remove from pan on to a paper napkin to absorb excess oil.
8. Cut into two triangles.
9. Serve hot with tomato sauce or mint chutney.

Walnut and Broccoli Soup

The very healthy broccoli, rich in calcium and anti-oxidants is combined with the omega 3 rich walnuts. Cinnamon has a soothing effect which relaxes the nerves.

Serves 4

2 tbsp walnuts - chopped
1 small broccoli - break into tiny florets (2 cups florets)
1 cup chopped spinach
1 tsp oil, 1" stick cinnamon
3 cups water
1 cup milk
1 tsp salt and ½ tsp pepper, or to taste
a few drops of lemon juice, optional

1. Heat 1 tsp oil in a deep pan. Add cinnamon. Wait for a few seconds. Add broccoli and spinach. Cook without covering on low heat for 3-4 minutes.

2. Add water and bring to a boil. Simmer on low heat for 5-7 minutes till vegetables turn soft. Remove from fire and let it cool down completely.

3. Grind walnuts with ½ cup milk to a smooth paste in a small grinder. Remove the walnut paste from grinder and add the remaining milk to it. Keep aside.

4. Grind broccoli and spinach along with the water into a smooth puree. Strain puree. Mix walut paste to broccoli puree. Boil. Simmer for 2 minutes. Add salt and pepper to taste. Remove from fire. Add lemon juice before serving.

Spinach Orange Salad

A delightful green salad. You can substitute spinach with lettuce too or use a combination of both. Fruit adds texture and taste to the salad.

Serves 4-6

200 gm spinach (choose a firm & fresh bundle with small leaves), 2 firm oranges

DRESSING
1 tbsp olive oil, 1 tbsp vinegar, ½ tsp light soya sauce
½ tsp salt, ½ tsp pepper, ½ tsp sugar free powder

TOPPING
2-3 almonds - cut into thin long pieces

1. Trim the stems of spinach. Soak the spinach leaves for 15 minutes in a bowl of cold water to which ice cubes are added. Remove from water and pat dry on a kitchen towel. Tear into big pieces.

2. Remove the fibrous covering from each segment of orange. Keep aside.

3. Mix all the ingredients of the dressing in a small spice grinder or with a whisk till the dressing turns slightly thick.

4. Toast the almonds in a microwave for 2 minutes or on fire in a pan till fragrant. Cut almonds into slices.

5. At the time of serving, pour the dressing over the spinach, toss to mix well.

6. Lightly mix in the oranges. Remove the salad to a shallow flat bowl, top with toasted almonds. Serve immediately.

Subz Paneer Jalfrezi

Paneer deliciously combined with a variety of vegetables to make a medley.

Serves 4-5

200 gm paneer - cut into thin long pieces
200 gm (3) carrots - cut diagonally into very thin slices
1 long, firm tomato - cut into 4, pulp removed and cut into thin long pieces
½ capsicum - cut into thin strips
15-20 curry leaves, optional
4 tbsp oil

COLLECT TOGETHER
½ tsp cumin seeds (jeera)
½ tsp mustard seeds (*sarson*)
¾ tsp onion seeds (*kalonji*)
¼ tsp fenugreek seeds (*methi daana*)

MIX TOGETHER
5 tbsp tomato puree
2 tbsp tomato ketchup
2 tsp ginger-garlic paste or 2 tsp ginger-garlic - finely chopped
½ tsp red chilli powder, ½ tsp amchoor powder
1¼ tsp dhania powder, 1 tsp salt, or to taste

1. Mix together - tomato puree, tomato ketchup, ginger, garlic, red chilli powder, dhania powder, amchoor and salt in a bowl. Keep aside.
2. Heat 3 tbsp oil in a kadhai. Add the collected seeds together. When jeera turns golden, reduce heat and add curry leaves and stir for a few seconds.
3. Add the tomato puree mixed with dry masalas and stir on low heat for 2 minutes.
4. Add carrots. Stir for 2-3 minutes.
5. Add ¼ cup water. Cover the kadhai. Cook on low heat for about 4-5 minutes, till carrot is tender, but still remains crunchy at the same time.
6. Add capsicum. Saute for 2 minutes. Add paneer and tomato slices. Stir to mix well. Remove from fire.

Tomato-Kaju Idli

A wonderful light snack, with the goodness of semolina.

Makes 6 idlis

1 cup semolina (*suji / rawa*)
1½ tbsp oil
1 cup curd
½ cup water, approx.
½ tsp soda-bi-carb, ¾ tsp salt

OTHER INGREDIENTS
1 firm tomato- cut into 8 slices
4-5 cashews - split into halves
8-10 curry leaves

1. In a dish put 1½ tbsp oil. Microwave for 1 minute.
2. Add suji. Mix well. Microwave uncovered for 2 minutes.
3. Add salt. Mix well. Allow to cool.
4. Add curd and water. Mix till smooth.
5. Add soda-bi-carb. Mix very well till smooth. Keep aside for 10 minutes.
6. Grease 6 small glass bowls (*katoris*) or plastic idli boxes. Arrange a slice of tomato, a split cashew half and a curry leaf at the bottom of the katori.
7. Pour 3-4 tbsp mixture into each katori.
8. Arrange bowls (*katoris*) in a ring in the microwave and microwave uncovered for 3½ minutes. Do not microwave more even if they appear wet.
9. Let them stand for 5 minutes. They will turn dry. Serve hot with sambhar and chutney.

Saag Murg

Chicken with greens is a complete dish. Just some bread will make it a whole meal.

Serves 4-5

1 chicken (700-800 gm) - cut into 8 or 12 pieces
500 gm spinach (*paalak*), 250 gm fenugreek greens (*methi*)
2-3 onions - chopped finely
3 tbsp ginger-garlic-green chilli paste
1 large tomato - chopped
½ cup thick yogurt - beaten well till smooth
1 tsp *garam masala*, 1 tsp chilli powder, salt to taste
½ cup milk or water, 4-5 tbsp oil
2 tbsp cream to garnish (optional)

1. Sprinkle salt on methi leaves and keep aside for 15 minutes. Squeeze to remove bitterness from the leaves.
2. Discard stems of spinach and chop the leaves finely. Wash both leaves in plenty of water, changing water several times.
3. Heat oil in a heavy bottomed pan. Add onions. Cook till light brown.
4. Add the ginger-garlic-green chilli paste. Cook for 1 minute.
5. Add tomato. Cook for 1 minute, till it turns mushy.
6. Add yogurt, salt, chilli powder, garam masala and cook on high flame or till oil separates a little.
7. Squeeze out all the excess water from spinach and methi leaves. Add to the masala. Cook on high flame till all the excess water evaporates.
8. Now add the washed chicken pieces and stir fry on medium high heat stirring constantly.
9. Cook till water evaporates and the masala sticks to the chicken pieces.
10. Add milk or water. Reduce heat. Cover and cook till chicken is tender.
11. Remove cover and cook for 2 to 3 minutes or till chicken pieces are coated with spinach masala.
12. Garnish with cream. Serve hot.

Breakfast Platter

Serves 2

PANEER BALLS
100 gm home made paneer (made from 800 gm/4 cups) skim milk) - mashed (1 cup)
juice of 1 lemon to curdle paneer
1 tbsp chopped coriander, 1 green chilli - chopped, ½ tsp red chilli powder
½ tsp dried mango powder (*amchoor*), ¼ tsp salt
1 tsp sesame seeds (*til*)

OTHER INGREDIENTS
100 gm fresh mushrooms - cut into 4 pieces
2 tsp oil, 1 flake garlic - chopped, 2 small onions - cut into fine rings
1 green chilli - chopped finely, 1 tsp lemon juice, ½ tsp salt
¼ tsp each of pepper
1 cup sprouts (*moth*) - soaked in hot water for 10 minutes
2 tomatoes, ¼ tsp each of salt & pepper

1. To prepare paneer balls, boil milk. Add about 1 tbsp lemon juice to the boiling milk to curdle. Add more lemon juice if needed. Remove from fire and strain through a muslin cloth. Squeeze gently and mash well. Add green chillies & coriander. Make 8 small balls. Mix salt, amchoor and red chilli powder. Roll the prepared paneer balls in it. Keep aside.
2. Boil 4 cups water with 1 tsp salt, ½ tsp sugar and ¼ tsp haldi. Add sprouts and leave them covered for 10 minutes to turn soft. Strain after 10 minutes.
3. Heat 2 tsp oil in a pan. Add onions and garlic. Cook till onions turn light brown. Add mushrooms. Saute on medium flame for 2 minutes. Add green chilli and sprouts. Stir for 1-2 minutes. Add salt, pepper and lemon juice to taste. Remove from fire.
4. Cut tomatoes into two pieces. Sprinkle salt and pepper on them.
5. At serving time, heat the pan. Put ½ tsp oil; slow down the fire, then put til (sesame seeds). Roast for 1-2 minutes. Do not let them turn brown. Roll paneer balls on it so that they get coated with til. Remove balls and place the tomatoes in the pan with the cut side down. Cook for 2-3 minutes on low heat.
6. Place some hot mushroom-sprouts mix on a serving plate. On it place the paneer balls. Place the tomato halves on the side. Serve immediately.

Achaari Broccoli & Kaddu

Serves 4

250 gm pumpkin (*kaddu*) - cut in 1" pieces
150 gm (1 medium) broccoli - cut into florets
1 firm tomato - cut into 8 pieces and pulp removed, 4 tbsp oil
2 large onions - chopped roughly, ½ tsp salt, or to taste, ¼ tsp turmeric (*haldi*)
1 tsp coriander (*dhania*) powder, ½ tsp chilli powder, ½ tsp sugar
½ tsp dry mango (*amchoor*) powder

ACHAARI TEMPERING

¾ tsp nigella seeds (*kalonji*), ¼ tsp fenugreek seeds (*methi dana*)
¾ tsp cumin seeds (*jeera*), ¾ tsp mustard seeds (*rai*), ¾ tsp fennel (*saunf*)
2 red chillies - broken in ½" pieces

1. Boil 1½ cups water with ½ tsp salt. Add broccoli and cook for 2 minutes till crisp tender. Remove from water and keep aside.

2. Collect all the achaari ingredients for tempering.

3. Heat 4 tbsp oil in a *kadhai* and add the achaari ingredients. After a minute, add the onions and cook till light brown.

4. Add salt, turmeric, coriander, chilli powder. Stir for a few seconds. Add pumpkin and stir fry for a minute. Add ¼ cup water. Cover and cook for about 10 minutes till pumpkin is tender but holds its shape.

5. Sprinkle sugar and dry mango powder. Add the broccoli and tomatoes. Mix well for 2-3 minutes and serve hot.

Spiced Paalak Roti

Makes 8

1 cup whole wheat flour (*atta*), ½ cup gram flour (*besan*), ½ cup bajra flour (optional)
1 tsp fennel (*saunf*) - crush to a powder
1 cup finely chopped spinach (*paalak*)
1 onion - finely chopped, 1½ tsp chopped ginger
1½ tsp chopped garlic, 1 tsp onion seeds (*kalonji*), 1 tsp salt, 1 tsp red chilli
1 tsp amchoor, 1 tsp ground coriander (*dhania*), water to knead

1. Mix all the above ingredients and form a dough of rolling consistency. Keep aside covered for 30 minutes. Make chapattis and serve hot.

Wheat Bran-Soya Roti

Serves 4

1 cup whole wheat flour (*atta*), ½ cup wheat bran, ½ cup soya flour

FILLING
2 cups grated cauliflower, 2-3 tbsp chopped fresh coriander
1" piece ginger - grated finely, 1 tsp salt, ½ tsp garam masala
½ tsp red chilli powder, 1 green chilli - deseeded and chopped

1. Mix soya, whole wheat flour and bran. Add enough water to get dough of rolling consistency. Knead well till smooth. Cover and keep aside for at least 30 minutes.

2. For filling, add all ingredients to the grated cauliflower and mix well. Keep aside for 15 minutes. Squeeze the cauliflower well after 15 minutes to drain out the excess water. Make a stuffed roti using cauliflower as the filling. Serve.

Vegetable Chaat Nuggets

Delicious nuggets with a crisp covering, similar in taste to the pao bhaji mixture.

Serves 4

1 cup chopped cabbage, 2 cups chopped cauliflower (tiny florets), ½ cup shelled peas
½ cup very finely chopped carrots
1 tsp oil
1 tsp ginger-garlic paste, 2 tsp pao-bhaji masala
2 bread slices- churned in a mixer to get fresh crumbs
¾ tsp salt, or to taste, ½ tsp sugar, 1 tsp chaat masala
1 tbsp lemon juice

COATING
½ cup suji, ½ tsp salt, ½ tsp pepper

1. Pressure cook cabbage, cauliflower, carrots and peas with ½ cup water to give 2 whistles. Reduce heat and keep for 3-4 minutes. Remove from fire and let the pressure drop. Mash the vegetables roughly. Keep the mixture back on fire and stir continuously for 5-7 minutes till the mixture turns completely dry.

2. Heat oil. Add ginger-garlic paste. Stir. Add pao-bhaji masala. Stir for a minute.

3. Add pressure cooked and mashed vegetables. Saute for 2-3 minutes; remove from fire. Add salt, sugar, chaat masala and lemon juice. Mix well for 2-3 minutes. Remove from fire and let the mixture cool down.

4. Add bread crumbs mix well again. Shape into balls. Flatten to get oval, flat nuggets.

5. For the coating, mix suji, salt and pepper and spread on a plate. Roll the nuggets over the suji mixture to coat well.

6. At serving time, pan fry in a non-stick pan in 1 tsp oil till golden. Change side and cook the other side too. Sprinkle some chaat masala and serve hot.

POST NATAL RECIPES

Healthy Measures After Child Birth

Be Active, Eat Well and Be Yourself!

Eating well after giving birth and during breast feeding is essential to replenish nutrient stores in your body.

Step 1: Wait for about six weeks after your baby is born before you begin any formal attempt to lose weight. This will give your body a chance to recover from the stress of pregnancy and childbirth.

Step 2: Eat iron-rich foods (especially if you are breast-feeding) and keep taking your supplements. This will help you recover from blood-loss during delivery.

Step 3: Try to eat about 300 fewer calories per day than you needed during pregnancy if you are not breast-feeding; this will help you lose weight safely and gradually. If you are breast-feeding, add 300 calories to what you needed during pregnancy.

Step 4: Be patient with yourself. It took 9 months to put the weight on, and it can take up to a year for your body to get back to normal.

Step 5: Keep your energy up by eating a healthy balance of carbohydrates and protein.

Step 6: Get up to 30 percent of your daily calories from fat. Some healthy fats include olive oil and avocados.

Step 7: Try to eat lots of whole grains, legumes and leafy green vegetables; these will give you most nutritional value with the lowest levels of calories & fat.

Some Tips...

- Try to combine foods containing iron with foods containing vitamin C, this will help your body to absorb the iron more efficiently.
- Keep moving. Exercise combined with a healthy diet will help get your body back to normal as rapidly as possible.
- Stay off crash or fad diets. Over dieting can send your metabolism into starvation mode and hinder postpartum weight loss.
- When breast-feeding, the extra weight you gained during pregnancy should come off naturally and fairly easily; don't go on any formal weight-loss without consulting your doctor.

Commonly Asked Questions...

Q. **Can I have caffeine drinks?**

Ans. Coffee, tea and soft drinks with caffeine should be limited. Caffeine does pass through the milk and makes some babies restless and fussy. Try decaffeinated coffee and tea and caffeine-free soft drinks.

Q. **Can I drink alcoholic drinks?**

Ans. Alcohol should be avoided. Alcohol is a drug and it does pass through the nursing mothers milk to the baby.

Q. **Are there foods I shouldn't eat?**

Ans. Generally speaking, you can eat anything you want to, in moderation. Most mothers are able to eat anything they want with no problems. However, there are some babies whose digestive systems are not fully mature, and spicy and gassy foods like pizzas, onions, cabbage, broccoli or beans might make them fussy. Try eating different foods, one at a time, to see how your baby reacts to them. If something really makes him fussy and uncomfortable, don't eat it for a couple of weeks. As his digestive system matures, he can handle much more.

Q. **After delivery can I start smoking?**

Ans. Heavy smoking (more than 20) can reduce milk supply and have a strong effect on the baby. Certainly the second hand smoke is most poisonous to infants and everyone should smoke away from the baby. You are still in the process of keeping your baby away from upper respiratory infections. For your own health, and that of your baby's, one should try and resist the urge to smoke again.

Porridge with Dates and Bananas

Cracked wheat is said to improve the flow of milk in lactating mothers. Instead of using sugar which has only empty calories, try using the nutritive dates for sweetening porridge.

Makes 2 bowls

1/2 cup cracked wheat (*dalia*)
1-2 dates - finely chopped
1/2 cup milk, approx.
a few slices of banana

1. Wash dalia in water 2-3 times. Add 2 cups water and dates.
2. Bring to a boil. Cook on low heat till the dalia turns soft and the water is absorbed.
3. Add milk and bring to a boil. Remove from heat.
4. Add banana. Serve hot.

Nutty Banana Smoothie

Serves 1

1 cup orange juice
1 frozen medium banana - cut into pieces
1 tsp peanuts - roughly crushed
1-2 tbsp honey

1. Pour orange juice into blender.
2. Add banana, peanuts and honey and blend until smooth. Pour in a glass and serve.

Spicy Vegetable Dalia

A fibre rich breakfast prepared from cracked wheat.

Serves 4

1 cup cracked wheat (*dalia*)
½ cup finely chopped beans
½ cup finely chopped carrot
½ cup finely chopped capsicum
2 tsp olive oil
1 tsp cumin seeds (*jeera*)
1-2 green chillies - chopped
3 cloves garlic - chopped
1 onion - finely chopped
¼ tsp turmeric (*haldi*)
¼ tsp red chilli powder
½ tsp coriander (*dhania*) powder
1 tsp mint (*pudina*)
2-3 tbsp chopped coriander
1 tsp salt, 1 tbsp lemon juice

1. Roast dalia with 1 tsp oil in a non-stick pan for 7-8 minutes, on medium heat stirring constantly till it changes colour and turns fragrant. Remove from pan and keep aside.

2. Heat 1 tsp oil again in the pan. Add cumin seeds. Wait till cumin seeds turn light brown.

3. Add garlic and green chillies. Stir and add onions. Stir fry on medium heat till onions turn light brown.

4. Add the cut vegetables and sauté for 3-4 minutes. Add turmeric, red chilli, coriander and salt. Mix well for 2 minutes. Cook covered for 2-3 minutes till vegetables are almost tender.

5. Add 1½ cups water, dalia, mint and ½ tsp salt. Cook covered for about 10 minutes on low heat till vegetables are done and water is absorbed, stirring once or twice in between. Remove from fire. Add coriander and lemon juice. Mix and serve hot.

Broccoli Mayo Wraps

One of the best vegetables, broccoli is rich in calcium, iron and many other nutrients. These quick wraps can be enjoyed as a complete roll for dinner or cut into pieces for snacks.

Serves 4

DOUGH FOR TORTILLAS OR CHAPPATIS
¾ cup wheat flour (*atta*)
1 tbsp oil, ½ tsp salt
a pinch of baking powder

FILLING FOR 4 WRAPS
1 small broccoli- cut into tiny florets
3 tbsp oil, 1 tsp finely chopped garlic, 1 tsp cumin seeds (*jeera*)
1 onion - cut into rings, 1 tomato - chopped
½ tsp coriander (*dhania*) powder, ¼ tsp *garam masala*
¼ tsp dried mango powder (*amchoor*), ¼ tsp turmeric (*haldi*), 1 tsp salt, or to taste
1 tbsp lemon juice

OTHER INGREDIENTS
3-4 tbsp ready-made sour cream or mustard sauce, 2 tbsp tomato ketchup

1. Mix all ingredients of the dough and knead with the required amount of water. Keep covered for 20 minutes.
2. Heat oil for filling. Add jeera and garlic. Wait till they change colour. Add onion rings and stir till soft. Add broccoli and stir fry for 2-3 minutes. Add dhania powder, garam masala, amchoor and haldi.
3. Add tomato, stir for 2 minutes.
4. Add lemon juice and salt to taste. When the broccoli gets done, remove from fire.
5. Make 4 small balls of the dough. Roll them into thin chappatis/tortillas. Cook them very lightly on both sides on a *tawa* (griddle) on low heat.
6. Spread some sour cream/mustard on each chappati, covering till the sides.
7. To serve, spread some broccoli mixture on the roti. Roll up the roti tightly. Seal the ends with tomato ketchup.
8. To serve, heat 1 tbsp oil and pan-fry the wrap with the tucked side down till golden on both sides.

Tomato Fish

There is no denying the fact that fish is a very nutritive, low calorie food.

Serves 3-4

500 gm fish - cut into 2" pieces
3 medium onions - chopped finely (1½ cups), 1 green capsicum - chopped finely
3 tbsp oil, 3 tomatoes - grind to a puree, 1 tsp chilli sauce, 1 tbsp vinegar
½ tsp sugar, ¾ tsp salt, or to taste, 2 tsp cornflour

1. Heat oil in a pan. Add onions. Stir fry till transparent. Add capsicum. Saute for a few seconds. Add fresh tomato puree, chilli sauce, salt, sugar and vinegar. Mix. Cook for 3-4 minutes till slightly dry.
2. Add fish in a single layer over the masala, without overlapping. Cook uncovered for 6-7 minutes on low heat. (Turn the pieces of fish after 3-4 minutes). When done, it is whitish from inside and is flaky when touched with a fork.
3. Remove the fish with a slotted spoon on to a serving dish.
4. To the sauce in the pan, add cornflour dissolved in ¾ cup of water. Give one boil. Simmer for 2-3 minutes. Pour over the fish. Serve tomato fish with rice.

Banana Berry Shake

Make the much needed milk more nutritive by the addition of these fruits. Strawberries are rich in Vitamin C and bananas are a good source of calcium and potassium.

Makes 1 large glass

½ cup cold milk
½ cup chopped strawberries (3-4)
½ cup chilled yogurt (*dahi*)
½ ripe banana - peeled & chopped
1 tbsp strawberry crush or jam
3 ice cubes
1 tbsp sugar

1. Put banana, strawberries and yogurt in the freezer for 20-30 minutes before blending the shake
2. In a mixer blend all the ingredients until smooth & serve immediately.

Egg Cups with Broccoli

Egg, a complete protein is complemented with broccoli.

Serves 4

4 eggs - hard boiled
2 tbsp spring onions - chopped very finely
¼ tsp mustard powder
250 gm (1 small flower) broccoli - cut into florets
1 tsp butter
25 gm (1 cube) cheese - grated (¼ cup)

WHITE SAUCE
1½ tbsp butter
1½ tbsp whole wheat flour (*atta*)
1 cup cold milk
¼ tsp each of salt, pepper, or to taste
2 tbsp cheese - grated (optional)

1. Boil 4 cups water with 1 tsp salt and 1 tsp sugar. Add broccoli florets to it. Boil for 1 minute. Remove from fire. Strain after 2 minutes. Heat a pan, add 1 tsp butter and saute broccoli for 1 minute till well coated with butter.
2. For the sauce, heat 1½ tbsp butter in a small heavy-bottomed pan. Add whole wheat flour. Reduce flame and stir for a minute. Add milk, stirring continuously. Boil. Cook till thick. Add salt and pepper to taste. Remove from fire. Add cheese. Keep white sauce aside.
3. Cut the boiled eggs into half lengthwise, remove the egg yolk, retaining the egg white cups. Mash the egg yolk with the fork, add about 4 tbsp white sauce, very finely chopped spring onions and mustard powder. Mix well.
4. Fill the egg white halves with the yolk mixture. Keep aside.
5. Spread 2-3 tbsp sauce at the base of an oven proof dish. Arrange the broccoli in the centre of a baking dish and surround with egg halves. Top the broccoli with the remaining white sauce. Sprinkle cheese on the eggs and broccoli.
6. Grill in a preheated oven for 5 minutes. Garnish with little paprika or red chilli powder. Serve with toasts.

Panjiri

It is a tradition to give panjiri to the new mother for a couple of months. It is believed to help her regain her strength after labour and child birth.

Makes 500 gm

2 cups wheat flour (*atta*), 1 cup semolina (*suji*)
1 cup *ghee*, 1½ cups powdered sugar, or to taste
¾ cup puffed lotus seeds (*makhane*), ½ cup gum (*gondh*)
¼ cup almonds, 2 tbsp melon seeds or *magaz*, 2 tbsp cashews, 2 tbsp pistachios (*pista*)
¼ cup raisins, ½ tsp ginger powder (*saunth*), seeds of 2-3 black cardamoms

1. Heat ghee. Reduce heat. Add makhane to the ghee and fry on low heat for 1-2 minutes till they turn light golden & crisp. Remove makhane from ghee.
2. Now add the nuts - almonds, magaz, kaju & pista to the ghee. Fry again on low heat till fragrant, for about ½- 1 minute. Remove from ghee & keep aside.
3. Add gum to the ghee. Fry till it swells and turns transparent, for about 1-1½ minutes. Remove from ghee.
4. Crush all fried ingredients (makhane, nuts and gum) together coarsely. Keep aside.
5. Add the flour and suji to the remaining ghee and fry for about 5 minutes on low heat till pale golden and fragrant. Add raisins, ginger powder and cardamom powder. Mix well for a few seconds and remove from fire.
6. Immediately add powdered sugar to the hot panjiri. Mix well. Add the crushed nut mixture. Mix well and let it cool. Store in a bottle for a month or even more.

Good luck and Best Wishes to You and Your Baby!

FOOD
FOR YOUR
BABY

Food for the Baby as per Age

0-4 MONTHS

Mothers milk is the best. If using formula (powder) mix it with boiled water.

4-6 MONTHS

Texture of food:

Semi-liquid bland purees, without any lumps. Peel fruits and vegetables carefully. Remove pips and strings. Steam or boil. Puree or sieve.

Some recommended foods:

Pureed carrots, apple, potatoes, peas, marrow. Well-cooked green beans, cauliflower.

6-8 MONTHS

Texture of food:

Food can be minced or roughly mashed adding liquid or yogurt. Give plenty of finger foods like sticks of raw vegetables and peeled fruit.

Some recommended foods:

Minced chicken or fish (poach and remove all bones), mashed egg yolk (no egg white), plain yogurt, wheat cereals, tomato (remove skin first and sieve), sweet corn, soaked and dried apricots.

8-9 MONTHS

Texture of food:

Chop food rather than mashing it. Give plenty of finger foods. Stay nearby when the child is eating finger foods to prevent choking.

Other good foods:

Minced lamb, pasta, mashed lentils, toast, home-cooked dishes, soup, (all cooked without salt).

10-12 MONTHS

Texture of food:

Your child is eating almost everything the family eats, chopped into bite-sized pieces. Continue to avoid salt in the baby's food. Salt your food at the table.

Some recommended foods:

Green vegetables like broccoli, green beans, cabbage, capsicum, whole peeled tomato, citrus fruits like orange and pineapple.

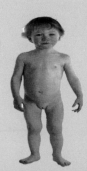

More About Children's Food

Q. How to reheat baby food?

Ans. Put the food in a small bowl. Take a bigger bowl with hot water. Put the smaller bowl in the bigger bowl. Let it remain in hot water till it comes to room temperature. Make sure the water in the bigger bowl does not get into the food.

Q. How to store baby food?

Ans. You can keep prepared food for your baby in the fridge for up to 24 hours. Always keep the food covered. After your baby has finished the meal, throw away any food that your baby's spoon has been dipped into, including commercial baby foods if you have fed her straight from the jar.

Q. Develop a water habit!

Ans. Many children never drink plain water, but have fruit juices or squashes instead. These drinks reduce their appetite but give no real nutrients. They contribute to tooth decay too. Offer water when your child is thirsty between meals. Colas and other fizzy drinks aren't suitable for young children, neither are "diet" soft drinks, which may contain high levels of artificial sweeteners.

Q. What to avoid...?

Ans.
1. Do not use any salt. Salt can damage young kidneys, and the child does not mind bland flavours. Salt should be started after the child is 10-12 months old.
2. Avoid citrus fruits, spinach, turnip, and beetroot before six months.
3. Avoid biscuits, cake, ice cream, pastry, fried foods before 8 months.
4. Avoid whole egg before eight months. Give only egg yolk at 6-8 months.
5. Avoid spicy, fatty, salty foods, sugary foods, fruit squashes, soft unpasteurized cheeses till the child is one year old.
6. Don't give soft cheese or honey under one year.
7. Avoid salty, processed, or fatty foods like salami, bacon, salt fish, Jersey milk, cream, and tandoori/barbecued foods till the child is four years old.

Recipes
4 Months - 1 Year

Upto 4 months, mothers milk is the best. If using formula (powder) mix it with boiled water. Start solid foods after the child is 4 months. The food should be bland as salt damages young kidneys. Serve food lukewarm.

Mashed Apple

4-6 Months

SERVES 1-2

1 apple
½ cup water

1. Peel apple carefully. Remove seeds and chop. Cook in water till soft. Mash with a potato masher. Sieve to a smooth puree. Add more boiled water or formula to make a semi liquid smooth puree. Serve lukewarm.

Suggestion:

A mixed fruit sauce can also be made, but it is always safer to use one fruit at a time and wait for a few days to see if it has any allergic reactions. Later as the child grows older, other fruits like pears, peaches, strawberries, plums etc. can be mixed to make sauces.

Banana Pudding

5-6 Months

SERVES 1-2

1 ripe banana
(the banana should be fully ripe)
4 tsp milk

FOR BABIES OLDER THAN 6 MONTHS
a tiny pinch of cardamom powder
2 glucose biscuits

1. Peel the ripe banana.
2. Cut into small pieces.
3. Blend into a puree in a blender or mash using a clean strainer.
4. Add warm milk and mix thoroughly.

Note: For babies older than 6 months, soak 2 glucose biscuits in hot milk so that the biscuits crumble completely. Add the banana puree and cardamom powder to make a tasty pudding.

Homemade Rice Cereal

Rice is normally the first cereal to be fed to a baby as it is least likely to trigger any allergic reactions.

5-6 Months

SERVES 1-2

¼ cup rice powder
1 cup water
½ cup milk (formula or expressed breast milk)
1 tsp sugar

1. Bring the water to a boil in a sauce pan.
2. Add rice powder while stirring constantly.
3. Simmer for atleast 10 minutes whisking constantly.
4. Add 1 tsp sugar.
5. Add the milk slowly and let simmer for 5 minutes on slow flame. Serve warm.

Note: You can add fruit purees (apple or banana or papaya) to make it more tasty and wholesome.

To obtain rice powder, grind rice grains in a blender or food processor.

Sooji Upma

Sooji suits the digestion and taste of a young baby very well. This is one of the two basic ways of feeding sooji to a young infant, the other being sooji kheer. Later, these recipes may be enhanced by adding a variety of other ingredients.

5-6 Months

SERVES 1-2

4 tsp sooji
1½ cups boiled water
¼ tsp salt
1 tsp ghee

1. Heat ghee in a kadhai.
2. Add sooji and bhuno on medium flame, stirring for 2-3 minutes till sooji begins to change color to light brown.
3. Add salt and hot water, stirring thoroughly on low flame till the right feeding consistency for your baby is obtained.

Note: After 6 months of age, you can grate half a cheese cube and add before feeding.

Sooji preparations become lumpy fast so it is a good idea to prepare immediately before baby's meal time and cool by stirring with a spoon at the time of feeding.

Papaya Puree

5/6 Months

SERVES 1-2

6 chunks of papaya
1 cup water
½ tsp sugar (optional)

1. Take 6 chunks of a fully ripe papaya.
2. Peel, de-seed and put the pieces in a pan.
3. Add water to cover the papaya chunks.
4. Gently steam (partially covered) on low flame till pieces are very soft. Use a clean strainer to puree the steamed chunks.
5. Add sugar (optional).

Note: Gentle steaming helps break down the sugars and fibres of the fruit for easier digestion by the infant. This need not be required after 7-8 months after which the puree may be obtained by putting ripe papaya pieces in a blender.

You can add 2 scoops of milk powder and 60 ml water (2 ounces) to the puree to obtain a yummy papaya smoothie.

Clear Moong Dal

Moong dal is usually the first of lentils to be introduced in an infant's diet. Once the baby gets used to this, other dals such as arhar or masoor as well as khichri can be introduced.

5-6 Months

SERVES 1-2

4 tsp dhuli moong dal
1½ cups water
¼ tsp salt
pinch of haldi
½ tsp ghee
few seeds of jeera
small pinch of hing

1. Wash the moong dal thoroughly.
2. Put in a pressre cooker and add water, salt and turmeric.
3. Put on medium flame. After 1 whistle, reduce flame. After another whistle on low flame, remove from flame.
4. Heat ghee. Add few (5-6) seeds of jeera and a tiny amount of hing.
5. Add the tadka to the dal. Mix thoroughly so that a uniform consistency of dal is obtained. Serve warm.

Note: Before feeding, the jeera seeds can be removed with a spoon.

Sweet Potatoes with Yogurt

6-8 Months

SERVES 1-2

½ small sweet potato
1 tbsp yogurt

1. Boil sweet potato along with the peel in water for about 10 minutes or till soft. Peel and mash.
2. Put ½ cup warm sweet potato in a blender or food processor. Add 1 tbsp yogurt. Blend to a puree, adding some boiled water/ formula or breast milk if needed to get a thick and lumpy mixture.

Suggestions:

For older babies, stir in diced fruit, such as apples, peaches or banana.

Mango Masti

7-10 Months

SERVES 1-2

1 ripe mango
½ cup plain curd
½ cup well cooked rice

1. Peel, de-seed and mash the mango using a blender.
2. Strain the mango puree to remove fibre threads.
3. Add ½ cup fresh curd and mix thoroughly.
4. Add the cooked rice and mix while slightly mashing in with a fork.

Note: Mangoes are usually introduced in the second half of the baby's first year. They need not be steamed as at this age, most babies can tolerate raw foods. However, if the baby's digestion is somewhat frail, mangoes too can be steamed and pureed.

Tiny dices of ripe mango make for a great finger food and can be fed as such to babies older than 9 months.

Semolina & Carrot Porridge

8-10 Months

2 tbsp semolina (*suji/rawa*)
½ of a carrot - grated
½ cup milk

1. Dry roast semolina in a pan on low heat for 2-3 minutes.
2. Add carrot and milk, cook stirring till it starts to boil. Cook for another minute.
3. Remove from heat. Brint to room temperature before feeding.

Lentil Khichri

8-10 Months

SERVES 1-2

2 tbsp rice
¼ cup split moong beans or yellow lentils
(*dhuli moong* or *arhar dal*)
1 tbsp finely chopped cauliflower
1 tsp oil or *desi ghee*
a pinch asafoetida (*hing*)
¼ tsp cumin seeds (*jeera*)
½ tsp fresh ginger paste

1. Wash rice and dal together till the water runs clear. Keep aside.
2. Heat ghee/oil in a heavy bottomed deep pan. Add asafoetida and cumin together.
3. When cumin turns golden, add ginger and cauliflower. Stir for a minute.
4. Add the dal and rice. Stir fry for 2-3 minutes gently on low heat.
5. Add 1½ cups water. Boil.
6. Cover and cook on very low heat for 12-15 minutes till the rice and dal is done and the khichree is thick and lumpy.

Rice Phirni

8–10 Months

SERVES 1-2

2 cups milk
¼ cup basmati rice (good quality rice)
3 tbsp mashed fruit (strawberry or apricot or mango)

1. Soak rice and then grind coarsely with 4 to 5 tablespoonfuls of cold water. Dissolve the rice paste in ¼ cup milk and make it thin.
2. Mix the rice paste and 1¾ cups milk in a heavy bottomed kadhai. Cook on low heat, for about 5 minutes, stirring continuously, till the mixture is of a thick consistency. Remove from fire.
3. Cool and add the fruit. Serve at room temperature.

Oatmeal and Bananas

10-12 Months

SERVES 1-2

¼ cup instant oats
¾ cup water
2-3 tbsp chopped banana

1. Combine the oats and water.
2. Bring to a boil, reduce heat and simmer for about 5 minutes. Remove from heat and stir in the banana.

Recipes
1 Year - 2 Years

Sprouty Peanut Tomato Rice

SERVES 2-3

½ cup uncooked rice - soaked for ½ hour
½ cup moong bean sprouts
2 tbsp peanuts (*moongphali*)
1 carrot - very finely chopped (½ cup)
½ cup french beans - finely chopped
2 tbsp oil
½ tsp cumin seeds (*jeera*)
1 small onion - sliced
1 tomato - pureed in a mixer
1 tsp lemon juice
1 tsp salt, or to taste

1. Heat 2 tbsp oil in a heavy bottomed pan. Add peanuts. Fry till they start to change colour. Immediately take them out of the pan. Pound them coarsely and keep aside.
2. Reduce flame. Add jeera, when it starts to crackle, add the onions. Stir-fry till light brown.
3. Add the sprouts and cook for 1 minute and then add the carrot and french beans. Cook for about 2 minutes on low flame.
4. Add the tomato puree and salt. Cook till the mixture is dry.
5. Drain the soaked rice. Add rice to the tomato mixture & stir-fry for 1 minute.
6. Add 1 cup water, bring it to a boil. Reduce heat. Cover with a very well fitting lid. Cook on low flame till done for about 10-12 minutes.
7. When rice is done, add the fried peanuts and lemon juice, mix lightly and serve with yogurt.

Corn Khichri

SERVES 1

1½ tbsp corn kernels
¼ cup rice
¼ tsp salt, a very tiny pinch of oregano
1 flake garlic - crushed
½ tbsp oil or ghee
1¼ cups water for cooking

1. Wash rice.
2. Heat oil/ghee in a saucepan. Add garlic. Stir.
3. Add corn and oregano. Stir well for a few seconds.
4. Add rice and salt, mix and cook covered on low heat till rice is cooked and the khichree is of a semi solid consistency. Cool. Mash well. Serve with yogurt.

Banana French Toast

SERVES 1

1 egg
½ banana - mashed
1 tsp brown sugar
a pinch of ground cinnamon
2 bread slices
2 tbsp oil for shallow frying

1. Whisk the eggs in a broad, flat bowl.
2. Mash banana. Add sugar and cinnamon powder to it.
3. Spread some mashed bananas on a slice of bread. Press another bread slice on it.
4. Dip the banana sandwich in the beaten eggs. Turn side after a minute so that the other side also gets coated with the egg.
5. Heat 2 tbsp oil on a non-stick *tawa*/griddle or pan. Spread the oil to cover the base of the pan.
6. Gently place the sandwich in oil. Reduce heat and cook for a minute till the egg gets done. Turn to cook the other side.
7. Remove from pan, cut into 2 pieces and serve warm.

Soya~Lauki Puri

SERVES 3-4

¾ cup wheat flour (*atta*)
¼ cup soya powder made by grinding soya nutri nuggets
1 tbsp semolina (*suji*)
1 cup grated bottle gourd (*lauki*)
¼ tsp salt
¼ tsp jeera powder (optional)

1. Mix all ingredients and make a dough by adding minimum amount of water. Keep dough covered with a moist cloth for 10-15 minutes.
2. Heat oil in a wok/*kadhai*. Make small balls from the dough. Roll out and deep fry in oil till puffed up and golden. Serve.

Note: This dough should not be kept out for a long time. However, it can be kept in the refrigerator for more than 24 hours.

Spinach/ Beetroot Cookies

MAKES 30
100 gm butter
60 gm powdered sugar
50 gm wheat flour (*atta*)
50 gm plain flour (*maida*)
2 tbsp raw spinach puree
or
2 tbsp raw beetroot puree

1. Sift both flours together. Keep aside.
2. Whisk butter and sugar until very light and fluffy with an electric beater.
3. Add spinach/beetroot puree to the above mixture and beat well.
4. Add flour gradually to the mixture and mix well to get a soft dough consistency, more like a thick paste.
5. Line a baking tray with brown paper. Grease the paper . Fill the cookie mixture in the piping bag. Pipe the desired shape.
6. Bake in a preheated oven at 200°C for 10 minutes. Let it cool down in the switched off oven for about 20 minutes, to become crisp. Serve.

Note: To make spinach puree, grind about ½ cup chopped spinach in a mixer to a puree. Similarly peel and grind beetroot in a mixer to get puree.

Savoury Vegetable Dalia

SERVES 4

1 cup dalia (cracked wheat)
3 tbsp oil, ½ tsp mustard seeds (*rai*)
½ onion - chopped
1 small carrot - chopped
2 tbsp green peas (*matar*)
2-3 french beans - chopped (optional)
½ cup tiny pieces of cauliflower
1½ tsp salt, ¼ tsp haldi
2 tbsp chopped coriander
1 tsp lemon juice

1. Roast dalia in 1 tbsp oil on low heat for 5 minutes till it turns golden and fragrant. Remove from pan and keep aside.
2. Heat 2 tbsp oil in a pan. Add mustard seeds, let them splutter for 30 seconds.
3. Add chopped onion. Stir for 1 minute.
4. Add carrot, peas, cauliflower & french beans, stir well for 2-3 minutes.
5. Add salt and haldi. Cook covered on low flame till the vegetables get cooked.
6. Add coriander and dalia and mix with the cooked vegetables. Add 2 cups water. Let it boil. Cover and cook on low flame for 10 minutes or till water is completely absorbed. Add lemon juice and mix lightly with a fork. Serve.

Paper Thin Veggie Chips

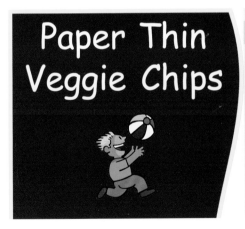

SERVES 4

2 carrots (*gajar*)
1 beetroot (*chukander*)
1 sweet potato or potato
oil for deep frying
¼ tsp pepper
1 tsp salt, ½ tsp oregano
2 tbsp cornflour

1. Peel all the vegetables, then slice the carrot, beetroot & sweet potato with the help of peeler into thin long slices. Pat dry all the vegetables on kitchen paper.
2. Heat oil in a big pan. Sprinkle veggies with cornflour and mix gently. This absorbs any excess moisture. Add the vegetable slices in batches & deep-fry for 2-3 minutes, until golden and crisp. Remove and drain on kitchen towel.
3. Immediately sprinkle pepper, oregano and salt over the hot chips.
4. Pile up the vegetable 'chips' on a plate and serve.

Fresh Chikoo Icecream

SERVES 4

200-250 gm fresh ripe chikoo
250 gm fresh cream
6 tbsp powdered sugar
1 tsp gelatine
½ tsp vanilla essence
2 tbsp raisins, preferably black raisins

1. Peel the chikoo and chop. Grind to a puree. Transfer to a bowl.
2. Soak gelatine in 1 tbsp water in a very small pan for 5 minutes. Stir on very low heat for a few seconds, till it dissolves.
3. Add gelatine to chikoo puree and mix well.
4. Whip cream with powdered sugar till thick.
5. Add chikoo puree to whipped cream. Mix well. Add essence and raisins. Mix and check sugar.
6. Transfer to an ice cream box. Cover with a plastic sheet (cling wrap) and then with the lid. Freeze overnight or till firm.

Potato and Pea Curry

SERVES 2

1 potato - cut into 1" cubes
½ cup shelled peas
2 tbsp oil
¼ tsp turmeric (*haldi*), ¼ tsp garam masala
½ tsp ground coriander (*dhania powder*)
½ tsp salt to taste

GRIND TOGETHER
2 tomatoes - chopped, 1 onion - chopped
2 flakes garlic, ½ tsp chopped ginger

1. Heat oil. Add the onion-tomato paste. Cook till it dries and oil separates.
2. Add the masalas - haldi, garam masala, coriander and salt. Stir for 1 minute.
3. Add potato cubes & stir for 3-4 minutes. Add 1 cup water & bring to a boil.
4. Add peas and simmer covered for 7-8 minutes till potatoes are cooked. Mash the potatoes slightly.
5. Serve with a bread (roti) or rice.

Cucumber Melts

MAKES 8

1 cucumber - cut into ¼" thick
slices without peeling
2 cheese slices - each slice cut into 4
tomato ketchup to dot

TOPPING
4 tbsp grated boiled potato
3 tbsp cheese spread
2 tbsp cream
¼ tsp salt and pinch of white pepper

1.   Keep 8 cucumber slices aside for use.
2.   Blend all the ingredients of the topping in a mixer to a smooth paste.
3.   Keep a piece of cheese slice on the cucumber.
4.   Place the topping on the cheese slice. To get a heaped look place 2 dollops of it, one on top of the other.
5.   Dot with tomato ketchup and serve.

Note: You could use a piping bag to pipe out the topping on the cucumber slices.

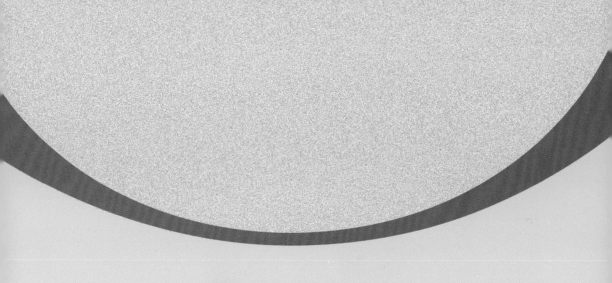

Recipes
2 Years - 3 Years

Baked Chick Pea Rounds

MAKES 12

1 cup chickpeas (*kabuli channa*)
1 tsp ginger -garlic paste (3-4 flakes of garlic
& ½" piece of ginger - crushed to a paste)
2 tbsp chopped coriander leaves
½ tsp salt, or to taste
some black pepper to taste
2+2 tbsp curd (thick)
1 tsp dry herb, (mint or parsley or oregano)
½ cup dry bread crumbs

FILLING
2 tbsp grated cottage cheese (*paneer*)
2 tbsp grated cheese
¼ tsp salt, or to taste

1. For the filling, mix paneer, grated cheese and salt. Keep aside.
2. Soak channa overnight. Drain water.
3. Add enough water to cover the channa. Add ½ tsp salt.
4. Pressure cook channa for 10 minutes or till soft. Remove from fire. Drain. Let it cool. Mash it finely with a potato masher or a *karhchi*.
5. Add ginger-garlic paste, coriander, salt, pepper and 2 tbsp of curd and mix lightly with hands.
6. Divide the mixture into 12 equal balls.
7. Stuff each with 1 tsp of filling (paneer-cheese mixture). Cover the filling to form a flat round cutlet.
8. Mix 2 tbsp curd with mint and spread this over the round cutlets. Sprinkle bread crumbs well to coat on all the sides.
9. Place on a greased baking tray or a rack covered with foil. Bake at 180°C for 25-30 minutes or until done.

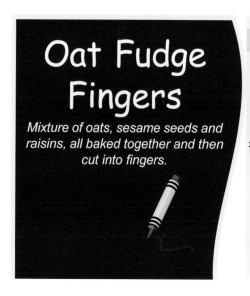

Oat Fudge Fingers

Mixture of oats, sesame seeds and raisins, all baked together and then cut into fingers.

MAKES ABOUT 20 FINGERS

¾ cup oats
¼ cup sesame seeds (*til*)
¾ cup brown sugar
2 tbsp raisins (*kishmish*)
¾ cup desiccated coconut (coconut powder)
½ cup melted white butter

1. Mix oats, sesame seeds, brown sugar, raisins and coconut.
2. Add melted butter. Mix well.
3. Take a small rectangular dish, or a square baking tin, or an aluminium ice tray and place a sheet of aluminium foil in it. Grease the foil with oil. Now spread the mixture on the aluminium foil to get a ½" thick layer.
4. Bake in a preheated oven at 150°C for about 15 minutes till light golden. Remove from oven.
5. Cool to room temperature. Then keep in the refrigerator for 1 hour. Cut into fingers with a sharp knife.

Note: In winter there is no need to keep the mixture in the refrigerator before cutting.

Vegetable Tomato Pasta

SERVES 2

1 cup whole wheat pasta or any other pasta
of your choice
½ cup chopped mixed vegetables
(cauliflower, carrot, capsicum, zucchini,
beans or peas)
2 tbsp butter
½ tsp garlic paste, 1 onion - chopped
2 tomatoes - pureed in a mixer
½ tsp sugar, salt and pepper to taste

CREAMY MIXTURE
¼ cup thick cream
2 tbsp cheese spread or cream cheese
3 tbsp milk

1. Boil 6 cups water with 1 tsp oil & 1 tsp salt. Add pasta. Boil for 10 minutes till pasta turns soft. Remove from fire. Drain water. Sprinkle 1 tsp olive oil on pasta. Keep aside.

2. Heat butter in a pan, add garlic & tomato puree. Cook till dry & oil separates. Add onions and cook for 1 minute. Add vegetables. Cook for 5 minutes till vegetables are tender.

3. Add pasta. Add salt, pepper and sugar. Cook for ½ minute. Keep aside till serving time.

4. At serving time, mix cream, cheese spread and milk together in a bowl. Stir into the pasta, cook for about 2 minutes. The cream sauce would thicken and coat the pasta. Check salt. Serve with garlic bread.

Egg Rolls

MAKES 8

4 eggs - hard boiled
¼ cup finely chopped onion
2 tbsp very finely sliced green beans
4 tbsp grated cheddar cheese
3 slices whole wheat bread - ground in a
mixer to get 1½ cups fresh bread crumbs
½ tsp salt, ½ tsp pepper
½ tsp mustard or 1 tsp mustard powder
2 tsp tomato ketchup, oil for frying

1. Grate the boiled eggs, add onion, green beans, cheese, salt, pepper, ketchup and mustard. Add bread crumbs.
2. Mix well. Shape into oblong rolls. Keep aside.
3. Heat oil in a pan and fry rolls, few at a time, on medium heat, till the rolls turn golden brown. Drain on absorbent paper.

81

Carrot Parantha

SERVES 2

¾ cup wheat flour (*atta*)
2 tsp butter or clarified butter (*desi ghee*)
1 carrot - roughly chopped
¼ tsp dry fenugreek leaves (*kasoori methi*)
¼ tsp salt, a pinch red chilli powder
¼ tsp carom seeds (*ajwain*)

FILLING
2 tbsp grated carrot
1 tsp finely chopped onion
a pinch of salt and pepper

1. Grind chopped carrot with a little water to a smooth puree in a mixer.

2. In a *paraat* (big bowl) put salt, kasoori methi, ajwain, red chilli powder, flour and carrot puree. Knead to a dough. Add water, if required. Make a smooth, soft dough.

3. Mix all the ingredients of the filling together.

4. Make small balls. Roll out a ball into a small circle. Put 1 tbsp filling, cover all sides and roll again to make a chappati.

5. Heat a griddle/*tawa*, put parantha on the hot tawa. When light golden specs appear on the underside, then turn side. Put ghee and fry on both sides till crisp and cooked. Serve with yogurt or butter.

Spaghetti with Chicken

SERVES 2

100 gm whole wheat spaghetti - boiled (2 cups)
100 gm boneless chicken - cut into thin strips & sprinkled with a pinch salt & pepper
2 tbsp butter, ½ onion - sliced
¼ cup grated carrot
¼ cup shredded cabbage
3 tbsp cream, 2 tbsp tomato ketchup
½ tsp salt, a pinch of black pepper
4 tbsp grated cheddar cheese

1. Boil 5-6 cups of water with 1 tsp oil and ½ tsp salt. Add spaghetti. Boil for 10-12 minutes or till almost done. Remove from fire. Let spaghetti be in water for 2 minutes. Drain when soft. Spread on a tray. Sprinkle 2 tbsp oil on the spaghetti. Mix gently. Keep aside.
2. Heat 2 tbsp butter. Add onions and chicken. Stir for 3-4 minutes, till chicken is tender.
3. Add carrot and cabbage. Cook, stirring for 2 minutes. Reduce heat. Add cream and ketchup. Mix well. Mix in the boiled spaghetti, cheese, salt and pepper. Serve.

Besani Bites

SERVES 4

1 cup gram flour (*besan*)
½ cup finely chopped spinach
1 tbsp oil
½ tsp salt or to taste, ¼ tsp pepper
½ tsp fennel (*saunf*) - crushed
½ tsp baking powder
½ tsp soda-bi-carb (*mitha soda*)
1 tsp lemon juice
green chutney or tomato ketchup to serve

1. Mix besan with spinach, oil, salt, pepper and fennel. Add about ½ cup water to make a thick batter of a soft dropping consistency. Beat well. Keep aside for 10 minutes.

2. Grease a sandwich toaster with oil. Add soda, baking powder and lemon juice to the batter and mix very well. Pour 2 tbsp batter in each mould into the heated and well greased toaster. Cook for 10 minutes till light golden.

3. Turn the sides to make the other side crisp too. Remove from the toaster after a few minutes. Serve hot with green chutney or tomato ketchup.

Hero Hot Dogs

SERVES 2

2 hot dog buns (preferably whole wheat)
French fries of 1 medium sized potato (do not peel the potato, fry fingers with the peel)
2 cheese slices - each cut diagonally into 2 small triangles
1 tomato - halved and cut into slices

MIX TOGETHER
4 tbsp ready-made mayonnaise
1½ tsp mustard or 1 tbsp tomato ketchup
¼ cup yogurt - put in a tea strainer for 10 minutes
2 tbsp grated carrot, 2 tbsp grated cabbage

1. Place mayonnaise, mustard or ketchup, and thick yogurt in a bowl. Mix well.
2. Add carrot and cabbage, mix well. Keep aside.
3. Cut hog dog bun into half, lengthwise.
4. Arrange the cheese triangles on the base of the hot dog bun.
5. Spread the mayonnaise mixture over the cheese.
6. Place the french fries and arrange the tomatoes over them. Cover with the top half of the hot dog bun.
7. To decorate, make a paper cone and spoon in 1 tbsp of cheese spread or mayonnaise and pipe it on the hot dog. Place a cherry in the centre, pierced with a tooth pick or tie the sandwich with a spring onion green. Serve with extra french fries and tomato slices.

Savoury Potatoes

SERVES 2

2 big, long potatoes, 2 tsp melted butter
2 tsp cheese spread or cream cheese

FILLING
½ cup boiled vermicelli (*seviyaan*)
2 tsp butter
1 tbsp chopped onion
1 tbsp finely chopped French beans
1 tbsp thickly grated carrot
1 tbsp chopped cabbage
2 tsp tomato ketchup
salt and pepper to taste

1. Boil potatoes till soft.
2. Remove the peel. Cut the potatoes lengthwise into two. Scoop out the centre. Keep aside.
3. For vermicelli filling, heat butter in a pan. Put onions. Stir. Add all the vegetables, vermicelli, ketchup, salt and pepper. Cook for 2-3 minutes. Remove from fire.
4. Fill the potato centres with vermicelli filling.
5. Brush potatoes on the outside with melted butter. Place in a pre-heated grill for 4-5 minutes.
6. Dot with cheese spread (optional). Serve.

Besan ki Burfi

MAKES 24 PIECES

250 gm (2¾ cups) besan (gramflour)
150 gm (1 cup) powdered sugar
150 gm (¾ cup) pure ghee
3-4 green cardamoms - powdered

1. In a heavy bottomed, put besan. Dry roast besan for about 10 minutes on low heat, stirring continuously till it becomes fragrant and gives out a roasted smell.
2. Add ghee. Cook on very low heat for about 15 minutes till the besan turns golden. Do not make it brown. Make it just golden with a hint of brown.
3. Remove from fire. Add sugar and mix well.
4. Transfer to a greased thali. Press well to make the top smooth.
5. Sprinkle illaichi powder. Leave to set for 5-6 hours at room temperature in a cool place but not in the refrigerator. You can leave it over night to set well.
6. Cut into 1" squares and store in an air tight box after it turns absolutely cold.

Atta Besan Laddu

MAKES 15 LADDUS

2 cups whole wheat flour (*atta*)
1 cup gram flour (*besan*)
1 cup powdered sugar, preferably *bura sugar*
¼ cup finely chopped mixed dry fruits
(almonds, raisins, kaju etc)
¾ cup ghee

1. Heat ghee in a kadhai. Add atta and besan. Roast on very low heat for about 15 minutes, stirring constantly, till the flour changes colour and gives out a fragrant roasted smell. Remove from fire.
2. Add finely chopped dry fruits in the mixture.
3. Add ground sugar and mix thoroughly. Make balls. Let them cool to room temperature. Store in an air tight box.

Pista Sandesh

MAKES 4-5 PIECES

1 litre full cream milk (5 cups)
2 tbsp vinegar, 2 tbsp water
7 tbsp powdered sugar or to taste
2 tbsp cornflour
2 tbsp pistachio - grind to a powder
a few drops of green colour

GARNISH
a few whole pistachio pieces

1. Boil the milk. Mix vinegar in water and gradually add it to the milk till the milk curdles. Strain the chenna in a muslin cloth. Dip the chenna packed in cloth in ice cold water for 10 minutes to stop further cooking. Hang the chenna in the cloth for 30 minutes to drain all water.
2. Grind chenna, sugar and cornflour in mixer till it is smooth. Transfer to a heavy bottomed kadhai.
3. Cook the chenna mixture for 8-10 minutes on low heat. The paneer should not change colour. It should turn dry and become thick.
4. Remove to a bowl, add powdered pistachio and green colour. Make round and flattened pieces. Decorate with pistachio. Refrigerate till serving time.

Oat Ka Halwa

A very healthy sweet treat for the growing children. A good change from the regular suji ka halwa.

SERVES 2-3

1 cup oats - powdered
6 tsp of desi ghee (clarified butter)
½ cup sugar
2 cups water
seeds of 2 green cardamoms - crushed
8-10 kishmish (raisins)
8-10 almonds - cut into thin long pieces

1. Mix water, kishmish, crushed illaichi and sugar. Boil. Remove from fire. Stir to dissolve the sugar. Keep aside.
2. Heat ghee in a kadhai. Fry oats on low heat till they just change colour.
3. Add sugar water mixture, stirring continuously for 3-4 minutes till the halwa leaves the sides of the kadhai. Remove from fire.
4. Transfer to a serving dish. Decorate with shredded almonds. Serve.

Nariyal ki Burfi

SERVES 10

250 gm dessicated coconut (*nariyal ka buraada*)
175 gm sugar (1 cup)
¼ cup water
250 gm khoa - mash roughly
2-3 drops or pinches of raspberry red colour

1. Heat a *kadhai* and warm khoa in it on low heat for 1 minute. Do not let the khoa change colour. Remove from fire and let it cool.
2. Heat water and sugar in saucepan. Cook for about 10 minutes till it forms one thread consistency. Remove from fire and let it come to room temperature.
3. Add dessicated coconut to the syrup. Mix well. Add khoa also and mix well.
4. Spread 2/3rds of the mixture in a small greased tray or a tiffin box. Add colour to the remaining 1/3rd part and mix well. Set it as the second layer on the white layer of burfi. Level it with the help of spoon and then keep aside for   1 hour to set. Cut into small square pieces.

Gajar ka Halwa

SERVES 5-6

1 kg carrots - grated
2½ cups milk
½ cup sugar
200 gm khoa - grated (1 cup)
4-5 tbsp desi ghee
some chopped nuts like almonds, raisins
(*badam, kishmish*) etc.

1. Mix grated carrots and milk in a heavy-bottom *kadhai*.
2. Cook for 20 minutes or more till milk dries.
3. Add sugar. Mix well. Cook till the *halwa* turns dry again.
4. Add ghee. Mix well. Stir till it gets well done and the *kadhai* turns greasy on the sides.
5. Add khoa and mix well. Mix chopped nuts. Remove from fire. Serve hot decorated with nuts.

GLOSSARY OF NAMES/TERMS

Arborio rice Italian, short grained, sticky rice.

Appetizers Small tasty bits of food served before meals.

Aubergine Brinjal/eggplant

Au gratin Any dish made with white sauce and covered with cheese and then baked or grilled.

Bake To cook by dry heat usually in an oven or a tandoor.

Batter Any mixture of flour and liquid, which is beaten or stirred to make a pouring consistency.

Beat To mix with a fast rotatory motion so that air is incorporated into the mixture. Beating makes the mixture light and fluffy.

Blanch To remove skin by dipping into hot water for a couple of minutes. e.g. to blanch tomatoes or almonds.

Blend To combine two or more ingredients.

Brinjal Aubergine/eggplant/baingan

Capsicums Bell peppers

Caramelize To heat sugar till it turns brown.

Consistency A term describing the texture, usually the thickness of a mixture.

Coriander Cilantro

Cornstarch Cornflour

Cream In sauces, half and half will do, in desserts use whipping or heavy cream.

Cut and fold To mix flour, cream or egg whites very gently into a mixture using a downward and upward movement.

To dust To sprinkle flour in an empty greased tin so that the cake does not stick to the tin during baking.

Dot To put a small amounts on top.

Dice To cut into small neat cubes.

Dough A mixture of flour, liquid etc., kneaded together into a stiff paste or roll.

Drain To remove liquid from food.

Garnish To decorate.

Marinate To soak food in a mixture for some time so that the flavour of the mixture penetrates into the food.

Plain flour All purpose flour, maida

Puree A smooth mixture obtained by rubbing cooked vegetables or blanched tomatoes through a sieve.

Saute To toss and make light brown in shallow fat.

Sift To pass dry ingredients through a fine sieve.

Toss To lightly mix ingredients without mashing them e.g. salads.

Whip To incorporate air by beating and thus increase the volume as in egg whites and whipped cream.

INTERNATIONAL CONVERSION GUIDE

These are not exact equivalents; they've been rounded-off to make measuring easier.

WEIGHTS & MEASURES

METRIC	IMPERIAL
15 g	½ oz
30 g	1 oz
60 g	2 oz
90 g	3 oz
125 g	4 oz (¼ lb)
155 g	5 oz
185 g	6 oz
220 g	7 oz
250 g	8 oz (½ lb)
280 g	9 oz
315 g	10 oz
345 g	11 oz
375 g	12 oz (¾ lb)
410 g	13 oz
440 g	14 oz
470 g	15 oz
500 g	16 oz (1 lb)
750 g	24 oz (1½ lb)
1 kg	30 oz (2 lb)

LIQUID MEASURES

METRIC	IMPERIAL
30 ml	1 fluid oz
60 ml	2 fluid oz
100 ml	3 fluid oz
125 ml	4 fluid oz
150 ml	5 fluid oz (¼ pint/1 gill)
190 ml	6 fluid oz
250 ml	8 fluid oz
300 ml	10 fluid oz (½ pint)
500 ml	16 fluid oz
600 ml	20 fluid oz (1 pint)
1000 ml	1¾ pints

CUPS & SPOON MEASURES

METRIC	IMPERIAL
1 ml	¼ tsp
2 ml	½ tsp
5 ml	1 tsp
15 ml	1 tbsp
60 ml	¼ cup
125 ml	½ cup
250 ml	1 cup

HELPFUL MEASURES

METRIC	IMPERIAL
3 mm	1/8 in
6 mm	¼ in
1 cm	½ in
2 cm	¾ in
2.5 cm	1 in
5 cm	2 in
6 cm	2½ in
8 cm	3 in
10 cm	4 in
13 cm	5 in
15 cm	6 in
18 cm	7 in
20 cm	8 in
23 cm	9 in
25 cm	10 in
28 cm	11 in
30 cm	12 in (1ft)

HOW TO MEASURE

When using the graduated metric measuring cups, it is important to shake the dry ingredients loosely into the required cup. Do not tap the cup on the table, or pack the ingredients into the cup unless otherwise directed. Level top of cup with a knife. When using graduated metric measuring spoons, level top of spoon with a knife. When measuring liquids in the jug, place jug on a flat surface, check for accuracy at eye level.

OVEN TEMPERATURE

These oven temperatures are only a guide. Always check the manufacturer's manual.

	°C (Celsius)	°F (Fahrenheit)	Gas Mark
Very low	120	250	1
Low	150	300	2
Moderately low	160	325	3
Moderate	180	350	4
Moderately high	190	375	5
High	200	400	6
Very high	230	450	7

BEST SELLING COOKBOOKS BY

Different ways with PASTA

Burger & Sandwiches

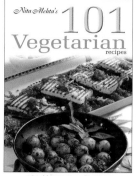

101 Vegetarian Recipes

Chocolate Cookbook

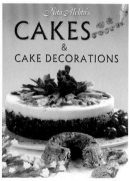

CAKES & Cake Decorations

Best of INDIAN COOKING

SPECIAL Non-Vegetarian Recipes

MEDITERRANEAN Cooking

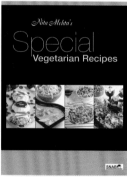

SPECIAL Recipes Vegetarian

Cooking for GROWING CHILDREN

Dadi Maa Ke Nuskhon Ka Khazana

EVERYDAY Cooking

MEXICAN cooking for the Indian kitchen

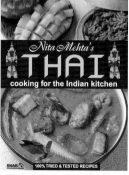

THAI cooking for the Indian kitchen

101 MICROWAVE Recipes

FOOD from around the WORLD

BEST SELLING COOKBOOKS BY

Fish & Prawns

Dilli Ka Khaana

CONTINENTAL cooking for the Indian kitchen

MULTICUISINE Cookbook

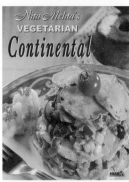

Vegetarian CONTINENTAL

Vegetarian SNACKS

Soups & Salads

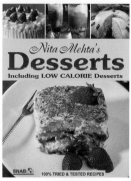

DESSERTS

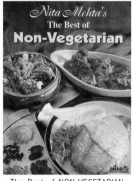

The Best of NON-VEGETARIAN

Vegetarian MUGHLAI

Vegetarian CHINESE

ZERO OIL Cooking

Different ways with PANEER

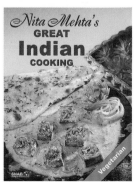

Great INDIAN Cooking

LOW CALORIE cooking for the Indian kitchen

101 CHICKEN Recipes

BEST SELLING COOKBOOKS BY

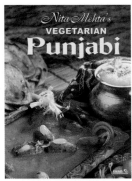

Vegetarian PUNJABI

CHINESE cooking for the Indian kitchen

ITALIAN cooking for the Indian kitchen

Simply Delicious CURRIES

The Best of CHICKEN & PANEER

SUBZIYAAN

TANDOORI cooking in the OVEN

Tempting SNACKS

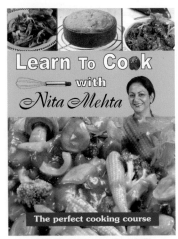

LEAR TO COOK with NITA MEHTA

Flavours of INDIAN Cooking

Oats Breakfast Cookbook

Leran to Cook CHOCOLATE

Learn Food Styling, Garnishing & Table Laying

Leran to Cook PIZZA & PASTA

Leran to Cook LEBANESE